MW01491241

Jesus
~and~ Proverbs

ISBN: 978-1-950791-19-4

Cover and text layout design: Kristi Yoder

Printed in the USA

Published by:

TGS International
P.O. Box 355
Berlin, Ohio 44610 USA
Phone: 330.893.4828
Fax: 330.893.2305
www.tgsinternational.com

Jesus

and Proverbs

Reconciling the teachings of Jesus and
Proverbs regarding money and business

Gary Miller

Table of Contents

Introduction

The Bible is an amazing book, managing to be both simple and yet complex. Written across centuries by men of diverse background, education, and social standing, it is obvious that humans alone could never have compiled such a manuscript. Its simplicity is evident in that even those who have little education can understand its message. Yet its truths are so deep that scholars spend their entire lives attempting to mine its depths.

Many of us have grown up blessed with easy access to the Bible. This is a tremendous blessing! Yet seeing it as a complete unit can sometimes give a false illusion of what the Bible actually is. We can subconsciously assume that the last of Jesus' disciples delivered a leather-bound document, similar to what we use, to the Early Church just before he died. We suppose that men like the Apostle Paul read his red-letter Bible every morning, complete with maps and a concordance, and naturally he would have preferred the King James Version. Obviously, this was not the case.

Our Bible is a compilation of manuscripts, letters, and facts of history that have been handed down through the centuries. The men involved in deciding which manuscripts to include in the final canon, as well as those who spent days copying manuscripts, were keenly aware that they were working with a collection of different types of writings. Yet we sometimes forget.

The primary purpose of this little book is not intended to address the way we read or interpret our Bibles. Rather, it is to address the different messages we find in the book of Proverbs and in the teachings of Jesus regarding wealth, possessions, and business. It is helpful to understand that our Bible is a compilation of different genres of literature—writings that need to be read in different ways and from differing perspectives.

After the book *It's Not Your Business* was published, I was encouraged by several individuals to consider making a small booklet out of the section titled "Jesus and Proverbs." They felt the information in that section was needed among our people, and regretted that it would be missed by individuals who would never read a "business book." This small book is in response to those requests, and portions of it have been taken directly out of *It's Not Your Business*.

My prayer is that, as you read, God will reveal more of what He has in mind, and that He will provide a clearer vision of how He intends for us to use our occupations for His kingdom. If you are an employee, may all those who come in contact with you sense that they have come face to face with someone who is purposefully laboring "together with God."[a]

---

[a] 1 Corinthians 3:9

And if you are a business owner, may your business demonstrate the beauty of kingdom Christianity to a lost and disillusioned world.

CHAPTER ONE

How Involved Should We Be?

"Jerry" was an unbelieving businessman in our local community who seemed to have an inherent knack for making money. He had a natural ability to see a need, develop a business to fill it, and make a profit in the process. As a young man I marveled at his capability, not only to operate his business efficiently but to continually expand. His father had owned a small gas station but had never seen the need to grow beyond one establishment. Jerry, however, was different. He couldn't understand why his father didn't develop the business. Why be content to own just one gas station in a city where so many people needed fuel. Why not expand?

Finally the day came when Jerry inherited his father's business, and immediately he began to act on his vision. Borrowing against the assets he had inherited, Jerry bought out another gas station in town. Jerry was a good manager and it wasn't long till he found ways to increase efficiency in the newly purchased station. Flush with profits from this new venture, Jerry began to look for an opportunity to repeat this process. Again and again Jerry bought gas stations that were not operating to their potential, increased their efficiency, and soon he owned a number of profitable gas stations.

Continued Expansion

As Jerry expanded, he began to look upstream at his supplier. Why not start his own fuel transport business? Why allow someone else to profit from supplying fuel to his stations? So Jerry began purchasing semi-trucks and soon had a fleet of trucks delivering fuel. Again, Jerry's business acumen and management skills created another profitable business. Now he not only owned many gas stations in this city but also the fuel delivery company that supplied them. But Jerry still didn't seem to be content. As he looked out over the region he saw many other gas stations that were flourishing, but the owners had no interest in selling. So Jerry decided to begin squeezing the competition.

Strategically, he would lower his prices at one of his stations near the station he wanted to purchase, sometimes even selling at a loss to attract customers to his station instead of his competitor's establishment. And it worked! The locals were only too glad to purchase at a lower price, and it wasn't long till some of these gas stations were willing to sell or go out of business.

As a young man I watched this take place and listened to the local people discuss this issue. Some were glad for the lower prices, while others seemed concerned about the methods Jerry was employing. They talked about the problem of monopolies, and used words like covetousness and greed. After all, what might happen if Jerry eventually owned all the stations in the area? Would gas prices remain low?

I worked at a construction site on one of Jerry's projects. One day my boss was talking to Jerry and brought up the subject. "Jerry, you have a large, successful business. Why not let some others in town own and enjoy operating gas stations as well? Why put others out of business so yours can keep growing larger?"

Jerry pondered this a moment before answering with a smile.

"Because I don't want *some* of the business or even *most* of it. I want to sell *all* the gas in this town!"

Should Christians Be Involved?

I was only a teenager at the time, but I remember being jarred by Jerry's comment. I was just a young believer in Jesus, but something about his statement caused me to question the compatibility of business and Christianity. Was this really what God had in mind? Even though Jerry wasn't a follower of Jesus, I knew many professing Christians who were heavily involved in business. Their attitudes toward business and wealth didn't seem much different than Jerry's, and I began to have questions. Was business, especially big business, something followers of Jesus should be involved in?

Many of us have wondered about this. We know we have been blessed, and we live in a country with tremendous opportunity. But we also recognize that our capitalistic environment has not always had a positive effect on the church. In some cases, we seem incapable of controlling business growth and, perhaps more importantly, holding the "successful" businessman accountable for how he uses his wealth.

Our conservative churches are capable of considering almost every imaginable topic. We discuss something, make a decision, and then hold members accountable. We know how to do that. But when we get to business and wealth, for some reason we fall strangely silent. It seems as though we don't know what to do with business. On the one hand we need to make an income, but on the other hand many seem to be more passionate about their businesses than about the kingdom of God. But must these two be in opposition to each other? Must we choose between being in business and following Jesus?

CHAPTER TWO

Three Men— One Church

While writing the book *It's Not Your Business*, I decided to take a survey. I wanted to find out what people think about business. Is commerce and involvement in the business world as we know it something God can bless? What about business ownership?

I designed a short survey and interviewed many people of different age and income brackets, choosing people who were serious about following Jesus.

My goal was to find out how they viewed business and what place they believed it should have in a Christian's life. I asked the following questions:

1. If you hear that a Christian businessman has 100 employees, is your first thought positive or negative?

2. Rate the occupational options below from 1-4 according to how you view them. Do you assume a man is more spiritual if he:

   a. ___ Is an employer?

   b. ___ Is employed by someone else?

   c. ___ Has a small family-based business and works at home?

   d. ___ Is a missionary?

3. Do you believe God calls some men to be foreign missionaries?

4. Do you believe God calls some men to be businessmen?

5. Can a man who is trying to follow Jesus in everyday life become the owner of a large business?

6. Can an owner of a large business meet his other obligations? Will it preoccupy him and keep him from being a good father?

Take some time to answer those questions in your own mind before you proceed. How do you regard business? As I interviewed people, I soon discovered that business, size of business, and business ownership are controversial topics. Some see business as a wonderful blessing, while others see it as something the serious follower of Jesus will avoid as much as possible. But I found that most believers fall into one of three basic categories.

Production Paul

Production Paul owns a successful business and sees his work as simply being a good steward of the abilities God has given him. He is perfectly comfortable with commerce and being part of the business world. He likes efficiency, organization, and making things work. In fact, he can't understand why more men don't have their own businesses; he suspects it is a result of laziness. Production Paul enjoys the challenges that operating a business brings his way and sees commerce as a source to fund relief for the poor and further the kingdom of God. He frequently speaks of the blessing of employment that Christian businesses provide. "Of course we need Christian businessmen," Production Paul likes to remind people. "It wouldn't be good if all of our men had to work in an ungodly environment."

Larry Little

Larry Little has listened to all of Production Paul's arguments, but he isn't quite so sure. Larry acknowledges that there are godly businessmen whose abilities provide a financial blessing to the kingdom. But he is concerned about men like Production Paul. Larry Little sees these businessmen start out with good intentions, yet over time they become ensnared, either by debt when things don't go well, or by wealth when successful. Larry likes and promotes home-based businesses where children can learn to work alongside their parents, but he is afraid of big business. He would like to see the church put some limits on how large a business may grow. Business, to Larry Little, can be a blessing when small, but very dangerous to a man's spiritual life when it grows too large. When a business grows beyond a few employees, Larry gets uneasy.

Servant Sam

Servant Sam has listened to the discussion regarding

business and has arrived at a different conclusion. He sees business ownership as dangerous and something to be avoided if at all possible. He has watched men with good intentions start a small business, only to become successful, make lots of money, and eventually become ensnared by wealth. These men had no intention of building a large business, but they were hard workers, found themselves in a good economy, and underestimated the power of riches. Servant Sam believes we are at times forced to become involved in the business world because we live on a cursed earth, but the less involvement the better. Because of his observations, Sam believes followers of Jesus should be servants, and never aspire to business ownership or financial success by worldly standards. Servant Sam cannot comprehend how someone could end up owning a large business if he is sincerely trying to imitate the life of Jesus, a man who didn't even have a place to lay His head.[a] Big business, to Servant Sam, is incompatible with the character of Christ.

Production Pauls, Larry Littles, and Servant Sams sit side by side on our church pews each Sunday.

---

[a] Luke 9:58

They nod in agreement when the preacher speaks out sharply against love for the world and money. They all shake their heads at the foolishness of materialism. They agree that believers are called to provide materially for their own families. Yet their views of business and how it relates to the kingdom of God are entirely different.

But they don't need to worry that their differing viewpoints will be exposed. The topic of business ownership, size of business, or how involved in business a believer should be is rarely, if ever, discussed during a church service. All three are free to carry their own opinions without fear of conflict. In many churches this topic is just too controversial to bring up. It is deemed better to just focus on safe "spiritual" topics and leave this issue of business and wealth alone.

But make no mistake! Even though there is little communication on this topic, each has a strong opinion on business and substantial evidence to support it. Their different gifts, personalities, and life experiences have helped create their worldviews, and each believes he is seeing this topic correctly. And, ironically, each is confident God shares his perspective.

CHAPTER THREE

Differing Perspectives

Most of us have been involved in a discussion when an opinion is offered regarding the accumulation of wealth, the size of a business, or how we should apply Biblical principles of stewardship. When this happens, it is amazing how people sit up and listen. In fact, it isn't uncommon for someone else to immediately offer another perspective or even an opposing view. Finances tend to be a hot topic and people have strong opinions. After all, money affects almost every part of our lives.

> Money affects almost every part of our lives.

So it is not surprising that immediately following a financial seminar or a message on finances, people tend to have questions or want to express an opinion. Maybe it was a statement that was made or a lingering question that wasn't addressed. And in my experience, people asking the questions can almost always be divided into one of two groups. The first group tends to be older, and I will call them the "Focus on Proverbs" group.

"Focus on Proverbs"

Many times the older gentleman will have some gray hair, and in the middle of the discussion he will say something like this:

"These young people need to go back and read what Proverbs has to say about diligence, saving money, and planning ahead. They need to learn from the ant! They just don't have the work ethic that people used to have. Many of them don't want to start a business or save for the future, and then when they get into trouble they come running to us older ones for financial help."

Expressions like this are common from the older generation. One gentleman even complained that some who are against savings accounts aren't even saving enough for their own funeral.

"Some of us who have been saving will need to cover the cost of their caskets!" he declared.

Statements like these typically come from older Production Pauls, and sometimes Larry Littles— men who have experienced difficult times. They have worked hard, created successful businesses, and now are asked by their church to mentor the younger generation—and, at times, shell out cash when there is a need. They become frustrated with the younger men, who often appear lazy and uninterested in saving money and providing for their own futures. They see the younger generation as ignorant of some basic common-sense teaching that Proverbs has to offer.

But these older ones are not the only ones who are alarmed. There is another group who is also disturbed. They see an older generation caught up in the business world and focused unduly on wealth and possessions. They are concerned when they see large businesses, second homes, and a heavy emphasis on "getting ahead." They don't understand how these older people can spend so much time and money on travel and recreation while the needs are so great in our world. There are exceptions, but this group is usually younger. I will refer to them as the "just focus on the teachings of Jesus" group.

"Focus on the Teachings of Jesus"

These people will say things like, "I don't understand the older people in my congregation. They seem consumed by business, getting ahead, and saving for retirement. Jesus told us clearly to sell what we have and give to the needy. He taught that the poor are blessed and that we shouldn't accumulate wealth. Yet some of our older church members are the wealthiest in our community. Jesus' words are not hard to understand. Why can't they just submit to what He said? We need more teaching on living out the teachings of Jesus regarding wealth and business."

Comments like these are common, and they usually come either from Servant Sams or from young men who are serious about following Jesus and have lost confidence in the older generation. They have watched some of the older men use profits from their large businesses or farms to indulge in a self-focused lifestyle, and they see these older wealthy men as blatantly ignoring some basic teachings of Jesus.

"It's Right There in the Bible!"

Quite often, we have these two opposing viewpoints existing in the same church fellowship. Depending on your age and experience you probably identify more with one than the other. But perhaps most amazing and unsettling is the reality that both of these groups use Scripture to defend their positions. Each can point to specific Biblical passages that support their perspective, as well as other verses that contradict the viewpoint of their opposition.

Before we really talk about these different perspectives on wealth and business, let's take a closer look at how we read and interpret Scripture. How is it possible for two serious individuals, both with a strong desire to obey the Word of God, to read the Bible and yet come away with opposing positions on a topic? My tendency, of course, is to assume that anyone who disagrees with my interpretation of Scripture isn't serious about following Jesus. After all, if they were really dedicated to the Word of God, wouldn't they come to the same understanding I have? I would like to think that my view, or the viewpoint of my church denomination, is correct and others are in error. But is it really likely that I and my fellowship are the sole possessors of truth?

Let's back up and take a closer look at how we read our Bibles. In fact, let's back up even further and look at some ways people have used Scripture to support some very illogical positions. Sometimes it is easier to identify errors in others than to see our own, and there are many examples of people who have used Scripture in erroneous ways. The Apostle Peter says that people in his day were wresting the Scriptures "to their own destruction."[a] We can be sure if it was occurring then, it is still happening today. We all need to ask ourselves the sobering question: Is it possible I am doing the same?

---

[a] 2 Peter 3:16

The Bible Says . . .

Most of us have met people who obviously interpret the Scriptures irrationally. They have a point to prove, so they find a verse that seems to verify their point of view. The way they are using the verse may be completely out of context, with the contrived meaning having no connection to the original message. But none of this seems to matter. The most important fact at the moment is that they have found a verse that says what they want. When our goal is to substantiate our personal opinion, or to prove our denomination more doctrinally correct than someone else's, we can become particularly adept at this skill. This is a great abuse of God's Word, yet it has been taking place from antiquity. In fact, history is replete with examples of misapplying Scripture.

Slavery Is Wrong

In the days leading up to the Civil War, professing Christians on both sides of the dispute used Scripture to validate their positions. Some risked their lives to hide slaves and help operate the Underground Railroad. They were trying to obey Jesus' command, "As ye would that men should do to you, do ye also to them likewise."[a] It seemed obvious that since they wouldn't want to be slaves themselves, they should do all they could to help people who were. They were aware that other verses taught obedience to civil authorities, yet they believed that if Jesus were living in their day He would help these slaves escape from oppression. And they believed they had Scripture behind them.

---

[a] Luke 6:31

Slavery Is Right

But the slaveholders used Scripture to justify their position as well. United States Senator James Henry Hammond explained his "Biblical" position on slavery like this: "The doom of Ham has been branded on the form and features of his African descendants. The hand of fate has united his color and destiny. Man cannot separate what God hath joined."[1] Senator Hammond seemed just as convinced as those who were hiding slaves that he was right. And he had found Scriptures to substantiate his opinion.

Jefferson Davis, president of the ill-fated Confederate States of America, also confidently declared, "[Slavery] was established by decree of Almighty God. . . . It is sanctioned in the Bible, in both Testaments, from Genesis to Revelation. . . . It has existed in all ages, has been found among the people of the highest civilization, and in nations of the highest proficiency in the arts."[2]

It is amazing that men professing to adhere to the same Bible could come out so far apart on this issue of slavery. But Scripture has been used to justify even more bizarre activities.

The Jews Should Be Persecuted

Few men are better known for their vile deeds than Adolf Hitler. Astoundingly, he used the Bible to justify his despicable deeds. In many of his speeches, Hitler used Scripture to vindicate his position, even using events from Jesus' life to demonstrate why it was perfectly right to hate and persecute the Jews. Consider these words of Hitler:

> In boundless love as a Christian and as a man, I read through the passage which tells us how the Lord at last rose in His might and seized the scourge to drive out of the Temple the brood of vipers and adders. How terrific was His fight for the world against the Jewish poison. Today, after two thousand years, with deepest emotion I recognize more profoundly than ever before the fact that it was for this that He had to shed His blood upon the Cross.[3]

It is hard to imagine someone taking the life and teachings of Jesus, the one who came to save His chosen people, and twisting them to this extent. But let's not pass off these historical misapplications as though the days of abusing Scripture are over. These men wanted something, and they went to the Bible to find a verse that agreed with what they wanted.

Scripture to Achieve Our Goals

Jefferson Davis believed in slavery. The economy of the South thrived largely because of slave labor. If all the slaves were suddenly emancipated, a tremendous amount of wealth would walk away, and the owners would be left with no way to operate their plantations. Therefore, in Jefferson Davis's mind, slavery must continue, and he went to the Bible to find substantiation.

Hitler hated the Jews, and annihilating them was his burning obsession. He knew that finding some passages that could be used for justification would help his cause. So when he read the Bible, it wasn't to find truth. It was to find validation for what he already desired.

As I read quotes from men like Hitler and Davis and observe the irrational ways in which they abused the Word of God, I have to assume you can find a verse to validate almost any doctrine, regardless how absurd. American Christianity can excuse almost any sin and find Scripture to justify it. You can find "Christians" who believe divorce and remarriage or going to war is acceptable, and they use the Bible to confirm it. Today many emphasize God's love to prove that He accepts homosexuality. Anyone who disagrees does not love like God does, we are told. And Scripture is used to substantiate this position.

As we reflect on our potential to twist Scripture, and as we consider what the Bible says about wealth and business, we should be sobered. All of us already have an opinion on this topic. Sometimes a fairly strong opinion! So in going to Scripture to see what God has to say, we must be careful not to simply come away with our own perspective solidified. As we have seen, we are very capable of going to the Bible and finding what we want! It is essential therefore, that we first examine our motives.

CHAPTER FIVE

Examining Our Motives

Joel Osteen, pastor of Lakewood Church in Houston, one of the largest churches in America, reportedly lives in a $10 million house and had a net worth in 2019 of $50 million.[4] His wealth, largely due to book sales, continues to rise. Joel views this as the blessing of God on his ministry. Joel is famous for teaching that God wants you to be wealthy. His first book, *Your Best Life Now*, remained on the *New*

York Times bestseller list for almost four years and has sold more than eight million copies.[5] It has even been made into a board game. Obviously his message of health and wealth resonates with the general public. Osteen teaches that God gives physical health and financial prosperity to those who are faithful to Him.

Is Joel Osteen's teaching Biblical? He quotes many Scriptures in his sermons, so it is definitely Biblical if you believe God is still working within the paradigm outlined in Deuteronomy. God's message was clear to those living in that time: Follow God and you will miraculously be blessed with health and wealth. You will get more rain, your crops will do better, and your animals will produce more. There are definitely Old Testament passages that support the health and wealth teaching.[a] There was a time when God's most obvious blessing was material prosperity.

If you focus on the teachings of Jesus, however, you will arrive at a very different conclusion. Jesus never encouraged the accumulation of earthly wealth. But no matter what Jesus said, the message

---

[a] Deuteronomy 7:12-14, 28:1-14

of Joel Osteen is popular and millions of people who buy his books would say that his teaching is directly from the Bible. After all, he quotes a lot of Scripture to back up his claims. It is essential, therefore, that we take a candid look at what we are looking for when we read the Bible.

What Am I Looking For?

As I take an honest look back over my life, I can see times when I was not a good judge of my own heart. Proverbs says, "Every way of a man is right in his own eyes,"[b] and I am fully capable of justifying positions in my life that are less than the best. As we look at controversial topics like money and business, it is essential that we understand this. If our hearts secretly desire to accumulate wealth, we will have a tendency to focus on certain verses while ignoring others.

We have an amazing capacity for justification. For example, we hear the Production Pauls say we need to develop large businesses so the profits can be used to bless others. But as we observe their lifestyles, this isn't always what we see. Even though the stated

---

[b] Proverbs 21:2

goals sound spiritual, sometimes a carnal and affluent way of life reveals other secret longings in the heart.

I have also observed the opposite. I have listened to Servant Sams, in reaction to the excesses of Production Pauls, focusing on certain verses while minimizing others. The desire to expose the "real" motives of the businessman can cause the Servant Sams to concentrate on verses that speak of the blessing of poverty, the danger of entanglement, and the warnings of Jesus to the rich. At the same time, they skip over verses that point out the need for diligence in material things. I have met Servant Sams who neglect hard work for "spiritual" reasons.

> Our desires and longings have a huge impact on how we read the Word of God.

Our desires and longings have a huge impact on how we read the Word of God. This is why Jesus warned, "Take heed how ye hear."[c]

---

[c] Luke 8:18

Neglecting Context

Inner longings also influence our interest in investigating context. When I find a verse that agrees with my personal views or desires, I generally have little interest in the context of that verse. After all, why research further? And this does not just apply to reading Scripture. If I have a low estimation of a brother and then hear some negative news about him, I am not inclined to investigate the truth of what I have heard. But if I deeply admire someone and hear a disparaging comment concerning him, I will demand evidence before accepting it. This is a tendency we need to acknowledge. Let's think about how this applies to wealth and business.

As you search the Bible for God's will in business involvement, you can find verses that seem to contradict others. For example, Jesus said a wise man will give thought and do some planning before he starts to build a tower.[d] That is only prudent. But He also said, "Take no thought for your life, what ye shall eat, or what ye shall drink."[e] Both of these

---

[d] Luke 14:28-32
[e] Matthew 6:25

verses are quoted by Christian teachers to support entirely different viewpoints. And if you are predisposed toward a particular opinion regarding business, one of these probably connects more than the other. So what are we to do? Is Scripture so vague that it allows for multiple interpretations? If the Bible can be used to justify the very thing it condemns, what good is it? The answer is both simple and sobering.

The Bible has the potential to provide whatever you truly desire. If a man is seeking justification for his path, then justification is what he will find. If he wants to prove that his denomination is correct, then that is what he will find. And just as surely, if a man is seeking truth when he reads, then truth is what he will find.

The real question is not whether there is a Bible verse that agrees with what you desire. The more important question has to do with the integrity of your own heart. When you read your Bible, what is your heart's desire? Is truth actually your ultimate goal? We must be willing to honestly ask ourselves, "What do I really want?"

But this doesn't completely solve the problem.

We also need to think about how we delineate Scripture. Does every verse, whether in the Old or New Testament, carry the same weight? Does context matter? Should the fact that a letter was written to a specific church with a particular problem be taken into account? Most of us would say context matters. We believe all Scripture is inspired by God, but we do not believe in a "flat Bible."

A Flat Bible?

In other words, we don't believe every verse in the Bible carries equal weight. If we are going to work through seeming discrepancies in the Scriptures, it is important to take time to understand the context in which they were written. Several verses in the Old Testament, for example, teach that stoning is the proper punishment for certain sins, while verses in the New Testament command us to love everyone, even our enemies. These are radically different teachings, and if we treated these verses equally, there would be endless debate.

Years ago our family was reading the account when Samuel came to inform Saul that he was to punish the Amalekites. "Now go and smite Amalek, and utterly destroy all that they have, and spare them not; but slay both man and woman, infant and suckling, ox and sheep, camel and ass."[f] Our youngest daughter, just old enough to grasp the severity of this command, looked up in alarm and blurted, "Does Jesus know about this?"

She wasn't very old, yet she comprehended that this was in direct opposition to what she had been taught about Jesus. There is no compatibility between "love your enemies, bless them that curse you, do good to them that hate you, and pray for them which despitefully use you and persecute you,"[g] and going out and slaughtering everything that moves. This was distressing to her. In her mind the Bible was flat, and everything we were reading was of equal value. Those of us who are older have learned that Old and New Testament verses do not carry equal weight.

Consequently, as we consider different passages of Scripture regarding wealth, we need to keep this in mind. Not only must our motives be examined, we

---

[f] 1 Samuel 15:3
[g] Matthew 5:44

also need to understand that context matters. We can't just pull out verses that seem to fill our need for the moment.

Years ago I was working on a construction project when the owner told several of us to come outside. He had hired a water witcher to find water on his property, and he wanted us to observe the process. I had heard about dousing for water but had never observed it, so I watched as the man talked to the broken-off branches in his hand, asking them where the water was, how many feet it was down to the water, and how much water a well at this location would produce. Chills ran down my spine as I saw the small sticks bend as though pressed by an unseen hand in response to his questions.

After he had finished, a couple of us challenged his involvement with water witching. We saw his activity as interacting with the forces of darkness, but he disagreed. He said he was a Christian and God had given him this gift and it was providing a good financial income for him.

"The Bible is very clear," he told us with confidence, "that 'the manifestation of the Spirit is given to every man to profit withal.' "[h]

I had read this verse many times but had never heard it applied in this way. And while he didn't convince me that God had given him this gift, I was persuaded of something else: you can find whatever you want in the Bible. This reality should sober us as we read our Bibles for direction.

In the next few chapters, we will look at some of the seeming differences in Scripture regarding business and wealth, especially between Proverbs and the teachings of Jesus. But it is essential that we really look for truth, because we will find what we are looking for!

[h] 1 Corinthians 12:7

CHAPTER SIX

The Message of Proverbs

Turn to almost any American "Christian" financial counselor's writings, and you will find a focus on the book of Proverbs. Take Dave Ramsey, for instance. While he would say money isn't the most important thing in the world, his teachings are unashamedly intended to help you accumulate it. Dave Ramsey grew up in Tennessee, and early in life he had an interest in financial management and wealth. By his mid-twenties he was a millionaire, enjoying a successful career in real estate. Dave describes his early financial life like this:

> Starting from nothing, by the time I was 26 I had a net worth of a little over a million dollars. I was making $250,000 a year— that's more than $20,000 a month net taxable income. I was really having fun.[6]

But he was also heavily in debt and oblivious to the potential consequences. As a result, when the local economy went south, he lost everything. This experience had a tremendous impact on how Dave viewed business and debt, and he began to read the Bible and other materials relating to finances. He also attended seminars and learned from Christian writers like Larry Burkett and Ron Blue. Soon Dave developed his own set of teaching materials based on his experience and what he had learned from others.

Today Dave Ramsey is a household name in America. His books can be found in most major bookstores, his materials are used in churches across the nation, and his voice is familiar on hundreds of radio stations. Using Scripture, he teaches people how to get out of debt, how to budget, and how to slowly accumulate wealth. It is a popular message, employing present frugality to enjoy future prosperity. "If you will live like no one else, later you can live like no one else," is Ramsey's familiar mantra, and millions of people are following his teachings.

But are Dave Ramsey's teachings correct? Are they really Biblical? His teachings have helped many recover from heavy debt loads, yet something about his message seems different than that of the Jesus he claims to follow. I want to suggest that Dave Ramsey's teachings are built directly on the message of Proverbs.

What Is the Message of Proverbs?

When considering business, industry, and wealth, the book of Proverbs has several clear teachings. So for a moment, set aside any preconceived ideas you may have about the problems regarding business and wealth in the church today and consider what the book of Proverbs teaches.

1. **Common sense.** Proverbs abounds with statements that we refer to as common sense. If you first do this and then that, the result will be this. "The

sluggard will not plow by reason of the cold; therefore shall he beg in harvest, and have nothing."[a] This is simply a true statement of common sense. If you choose to stay in the warm house and sleep in when you should be working in the field, you won't have a harvest. The book of Proverbs is packed with this kind of profound statements. It is a collection of natural, observable truths about life.

2. Self-preservation. Throughout the book of Proverbs the reader is taught to be diligent lest he be taken advantage of or lose what he has. Notice the underlying message of the following two verses: "Be not thou one of them that strike hands, or of them that are surety for debts. If thou hast nothing to pay, why should he take away thy bed from under thee?"[b] These verses apply to what is called co-signing for a loan, when one person pledges to share the risk with someone else. But notice the message. "Why would you do that? Why take that kind of risk? If the fellow you are co-signing the note for goes belly up, you might lose your own bed!" This underlying thought

---

[a] Proverbs 20:4
[b] Proverbs 22:26-27

pervades Proverbs. In essence, it teaches that there are consequences to choices we make in life. Don't make choices that might cause you to perish, to fall into mischief, or to be led into poverty. If you want to be successful, there are some things you should do and others you shouldn't.

3. Prosperity is the reward of diligence and frugality. "He that tilleth his land shall have plenty of bread: but he that followeth after vain persons shall have poverty enough."[c] This message is interwoven throughout the book. If you work hard and are diligent, you will be prosperous. Proverbs also warns against seeking wealth by other means. "Wealth gotten by vanity shall be diminished: but he that gathereth by labour shall increase."[d] The path to prosperity is taught clearly in Proverbs. "He that loveth pleasure shall be a poor man: he that loveth wine and oil shall not be rich."[e] The man who chooses to spend money on pleasure, living it up as he goes, will never accumulate much wealth. The path to wealth is hard work and a frugal lifestyle. It was

---

[c] Proverbs 28:19

[d] Proverbs 13:11 (also see Proverbs 20:21 regarding receiving an inheritance)

[e] Proverbs 21:17

true when Proverbs was written, and it is still true today. Material prosperity is the reward of diligence and frugality.

4. Poverty is the reward of slothfulness. The writer of Proverbs describes some things he observed while taking a walk. "I went by the field of the slothful, and by the vineyard of the man void of understanding; and, lo, it was all grown over with thorns, and nettles had covered the face thereof, and the stone wall thereof was broken down. Then I saw, and considered it well: I looked upon it, and received instruction. Yet a little sleep, a little slumber, a little folding of the hands to sleep: So shall thy poverty come as one that travelleth; and thy want as an armed man."[f] This is another recurring theme in the book of Proverbs. Material poverty is the result of poor choices, laziness, and slothfulness. If you are going to extract food and blessing out of this cursed earth, you will have to work for it. It will not come easily. Just as diligence and frugality have a reward, so does laziness. And the reward for slothfulness is poverty.

5. Planning and saving for the future. In Proverbs

---

[f] Proverbs 24:30-34

the lowly ant is held up as an example. "Go to the ant, thou sluggard; consider her ways, and be wise: which having no guide, overseer, or ruler, provideth her meat in the summer, and gathereth her food in the harvest."[g] Notice the ant is not only a diligent worker, but it also plans ahead. God has placed within the ant the knowledge that summer doesn't last forever. So while there is plenty, the ant gathers and saves for the coming winter. The lesson here is evident. A wise man knows that if he is going to succeed materially, he will need to plan ahead and save during times of plenty.

6. Material wealth is a blessing from God. Proverbs also shares some of the blessings of being rich. "The poor is hated even of his own neighbour: but the rich hath many friends."[h] This verse along with others says that a man who is wealthy will have more friends. Material wealth also provides some earthly security. "The rich man's wealth is his strong city: the destruction of the poor is their poverty."[i] The rich man is able to defend himself against many

---

[g] Proverbs 6:6-8
[h] Proverbs 14:20; 19:4
[i] Proverbs 10:15

things in life, another advantage to having wealth. Different characters in the Old Testament, whom we hold up today as righteous men, were very wealthy. I believe this is a fulfillment of God's promise. One verse in Proverbs says it like this: "The crown of the wise is their riches."[j] Wealth in the Old Testament seemed to provide some evidence that a man was approved by God. Of course, there were exceptions. There were poor widows who were faithful to God and wealthy men who were ungodly. But in general, wealth and prosperity were signs of God's blessing.

Many professing Christians are excited about Dave Ramsey's message. His books have been bestsellers, and many would say his message has saved their finances and marriages. But others are not so sure. Does God really intend for New Testament Christians to purposefully accumulate wealth? Are large businesses in our day really a sign of God's blessing? Is the book of Proverbs really the last word in financial teaching?

Dave Ramsey isn't the only one who likes to camp

---

[j] Proverbs 14:24

out in the teachings of Proverbs. Production Pauls, even those in conservative churches, like Proverbs too. One minister who owns a large company told me recently, "I read a chapter from it every morning. I have learned far more about running a business from the book of Proverbs than from all the business seminars I have attended." Proverbs does a good job of illustrating the importance of sound decision-making in business. Not only that, Proverbs provides a road map for accumulating material wealth. No wonder wealthy businessmen like it. It validates the path they have taken. But before we conclude that Proverbs is the last word in kingdom-focused living, we need to investigate further. What does the New Testament teach? What did Jesus Himself say on this topic?

CHAPTER SEVEN

What Did Jesus Say?

Throughout history, the Jewish people have been famous for their business acumen. Probably no people group is better known for skills in business, commerce, and the banking world. When Jesus taught the message we call the Sermon on the Mount, I don't think His listeners were expecting a lesson on finances. Yet Jesus dove right into the topics of wealth and possessions, and I think it is safe to say that, regardless of their financial status, everyone was surprised at His message.

What Is Jesus' Message?

In the last chapter we looked at what the book of Proverbs has to say regarding business and wealth. The Jewish listeners had heard these teachings all their lives. As we look at a summary of what Jesus had to say, consider how shocking His message would have been.

1. Common sense is lacking. One of the first attributes we see in Jesus' message on economics is an apparent lack of what we call common sense. Notice these words: "Give to him that asketh of thee, and from him that would borrow of thee turn not thou away."[a] Does that sound like common sense to you? Have you ever read anything like this in a "how to run a successful business" book or heard anything like this promoted in a wealth management seminar? And what about this one? "And if ye lend to them of whom ye hope to receive, what thank have ye? For sinners also lend to sinners, to receive as much again. But love ye your enemies, and do good, and lend, hoping for nothing

---

[a] Matthew 5:42

again."[b] Can you imagine a bank or credit union operating like this? These statements seem to fly in the face of common sense. I wonder what expressions were on the faces of Jesus' listeners that day. Can't you just imagine the thoughts racing through the minds of those who had a business? *That's foolishness! If I actually did that, what would happen to my business?*

If we're honest, we have had the same thoughts.

2. Self-denial is encouraged. Our natural tendency has always been to look out for ourselves. Self-preservation is a normal human focus. Here again the teachings of Jesus are revolutionary. "And as ye would that men should do to you, do ye also to them likewise."[c] Can't you see the wealthy merchant scratching his head? His goal had always been to convince people they needed his product. Wasn't that what a good salesman was supposed to do? But Jesus was saying that instead of selfishly trying to increase sales to maximize profits, the merchant should look at transactions from the buyer's point of view. That was a new thought!

Perhaps a building contractor who was competitively

---

[b] Luke 6:34, 35
[c] Luke 6:31

bidding on a project heard Jesus' statement. If he had discovered some way he could do the project more efficiently, should he share this information with his competitors? How could a man successfully run a business if he operated like that?

3. Prosperity is a great danger and potential snare. "Woe unto you that are rich!" Jesus said. "Ye have received your consolation."[d] I suspect the prosperous businessmen were a little shocked by this statement. They weren't used to being reprimanded. After all, they were the industrious ones, the ones people came to when they had a need. They had always looked up to wealthy patriarchs like Job, David, and Solomon and may have imagined themselves as modern-day Abrahams.

Jesus addressed prosperity repeatedly, and His message was consistent: Earthly wealth is a great danger and a potential snare to man. Later in His ministry He again warned against wealth. "How hardly shall they that have riches enter into the kingdom of God! For it is easier for a camel to go through a needle's eye, than

---

[d] Luke 6:24

for a rich man to enter into the kingdom of God."[e] This was so radically different that even the disciples, who were mostly poor men, were shocked. The Bible says they were "exceedingly amazed."[f] This was not the message they had been hearing from their culture or from the rabbi in the synagogue. This was entirely new!

4. Material poverty is a place of potential blessing. "And he lifted up his eyes on his disciples, and said, Blessed be ye poor: for yours is the kingdom of God."[g] And then, lest anyone be uncertain of what He was saying, Jesus continued, "Blessed are ye that hunger now: for ye shall be filled."[h] If anyone in the crowd hadn't been surprised yet, this statement would surely have done it. The poor and hungry are blessed? What was that supposed to mean?

While we want to be careful when interpreting the teachings of Jesus, I think we can say with confidence that God doesn't take pleasure in seeing people go hungry. Just a few chapters later we find Jesus so concerned about His hungry followers that He performed

---

[e] Luke 18:24, 25
[f] Matthew 19:25
[g] Luke 6:20
[h] Luke 6:21

a miracle so they could eat. This shows that when He spoke of the blessings of being poor and hungry, Jesus was exposing one of the snares of earthly wealth. Riches cause us to forget God and depend less on Him. A rich man depends on his wealth for deliverance in time of trouble, while a poor man tends to turn to God. For this reason, material poverty is a place of potential spiritual blessing.

> **Riches cause us to forget God and depend less on Him.**

5. Worrying about the future is discouraged. "Therefore I say unto you, Take no thought for your life, what ye shall eat, or what ye shall drink; nor yet for your body, what ye shall put on. Is not the life more than meat, and the body than raiment? Behold the fowls of the air: for they sow not, neither do they reap, nor gather into barns; yet your heavenly Father feedeth them. Are ye not much better than they?"[i] Businessmen are notorious for planning, plotting, and trying to peer into the future. Almost every financial

---

[i] Matthew 6:25, 26

seminar devotes part of the lecture to planning. Was Jesus really saying not to even think about the future? Was He contradicting His teaching on the importance of sitting down and counting the cost before starting a building project?[j] I don't think so. Instead, I believe He was teaching the foolishness of worrying about the future. The English Standard Version of the Bible says: "Therefore I tell you, do not be anxious about your life, what you will eat or what you will drink, nor about your body, what you will put on."[k]

Maybe we cross that line in business, and perhaps the larger the business the greater the tendency. I have repeatedly found myself lying in bed working through some business challenge, worrying what might happen if a bid was too low (or too high), or anxiously planning for an upcoming meeting with a disgruntled customer. We justify this anxiousness as part of normal business management. But the message of Jesus is that we are to release our fears of the future and turn this anxiety over to Him. This allows us to keep our focus where it needs to be.

---

[j] Luke 14:28-30
[k] Matthew 6:25 (ESV)

6. Storing in unsecured places is condemned. "Lay not up for yourselves treasures upon earth, where moth and rust doth corrupt, and where thieves break through and steal."[1] This revolutionary statement surely raised some eyebrows, and it is a message we too quickly gloss over. We hurriedly come up with all kinds of rationale for why it is important to save for the future. But why would Jesus have spoken these words if He didn't want us to obey them? Couldn't He have worded it a little differently? Our Father doesn't intend for His children to trust in earthly treasure, and Jesus goes on to say that "where your treasure is, there will your heart be also." A man who has stockpiled treasure on earth will find his mind swiftly going there when difficulty comes. Man cannot separate his treasure from his heart.

But Jesus taught that another problem exists with accumulating and storing material wealth on earth—there aren't any safe locations. If we're not supposed to store up treasures on earth because it isn't safe, what are we supposed to do? Where should a man stockpile his wealth?

Jesus didn't leave us without answers to these

---

[1] Matthew 6:19

questions. He went on to say, "But lay up for yourselves treasures in heaven, where neither moth nor rust doth corrupt, and where thieves do not break through nor steal."[m] In Luke 12 Jesus gives more detailed instructions, telling us exactly how to invest our wealth. "Sell that ye have, and give alms; provide yourselves bags which wax not old, a treasure in the heavens that faileth not, where no thief approacheth, neither moth corrupteth."[n]

If you want to be absolutely sure you are investing your money in a secure location, give it to the poor. Jesus gave the same message to another businessman one day, and it didn't go over very well. We know him as the rich young ruler. Jesus told him, "If thou wilt be perfect, go and sell that thou hast, and give to the poor, and thou shalt have treasure in heaven: and come and follow me."[o] This man had difficulty with Jesus' teaching, and many of us do too. We, like him, would like to keep our hands on our treasure while also ensuring its safety. But Jesus was crystal clear. There isn't a place on earth outside the risk

---

[m] Matthew 6:20

[n] Luke 12:33

[o] Matthew 19:21

of loss from moth, rust, or thieves! God wants His resources stored in a safe location.

Jesus didn't leave us very many words, and His total public ministry spanned only a few years. Yet centuries have passed and we still wrestle with His teachings. His words reach down into the recesses of our hearts (and wallets), and we can't help but wonder why He didn't use a little softer wording here or a little more explanation there. Did He really intend that businesses try to apply His teachings and operate using His message? Could a business even survive doing this?

If you are involved in business and are a Bible reader, these questions have gone through your mind. And if you are serious about following Jesus, you must answer them. But before we dive into whether or not Jesus would go broke trying to run a business today, we need to take a closer look at the book of Proverbs and the teachings of Jesus. Is it possible to reconcile the differences in their messages?

CHAPTER EIGHT

Understanding the Differences

I f we are honest, we must admit there are major differences between Proverbs and the teachings of Jesus. The overriding message in Proverbs is that a wise man works hard, plans ahead, saves for the future, is honest in his business dealings, and over time discovers that God's ways work. A man who continues down this path will eventually enjoy material prosperity, which is evidence that he is following

God's common-sense instructions.

In contrast, Jesus repeatedly teaches the blessing of being poor and the foolishness of focusing on material things. He reminds us that material wealth is a great snare, and emphasizes the superiority of eternal and unseen treasures compared to temporal material wealth. If we do accumulate earthly wealth, we are to sell it and give it to the poor. In other words, we need to exchange earthly treasure as quickly as possible for the wealth that is eternal.

Christian financial counselors and business planners use both the teachings of Jesus and the book of Proverbs. There is nothing wrong with this. But they (and we) need to be careful in reconciling their differences.

I am concerned when Christian financial counselors treat Proverbs and the words of Jesus equally in their teaching and writing. But we don't need to look outside our conservative churches to find this. Most of us have been guilty of this at some point. If we want to emphasize the importance of giving or putting God first in our lives, we might use a teaching of Jesus like, "Seek ye first the kingdom of God, and his righteousness, and all these things shall be added unto you."[a] But if we want to teach things like how to accumulate wealth, the importance of defending possessions and protecting against loss, or the many blessings of financial prosperity (as if we need to be taught!), we go to Proverbs. The Bible becomes a big pool of verses, and we just dip in and find the passage that says what we want.

Complete Honesty

As we try to reconcile Jesus' teachings and Proverbs, we must be honest about our goal. Am I a Production Paul with an overriding goal of having a large business and being successful by the world's standards? I see all these men who could be owning their own businesses, hiring more of our young men, and producing more revenue for the kingdom. It is frustrating to see all the lost opportunity!

Or maybe I am a Servant Sam who struggles financially and is frustrated by the wealthy men in my church. They own large businesses and place too much emphasis on working hard to get ahead. How I would love to show them some passages denouncing wealth so those Production Pauls could see their

---

[a] Matthew 6:33

error. After all, watching them head off on yet another vacation can be extremely irritating!

Whatever our goals when we read the Bible, there are verses that can provide justification—or ammunition. So let's stop for a moment and analyze our motives. Men who study the Word of God usually find what they are searching for. Let's begin by looking at what proverbs are.

> Men who study the Word of God usually find what they are searching for.

Proverbs

It is essential to consider the definitions of terms. A proverb, according to the dictionary, is a "brief, simple, and popular saying, or a phrase that gives advice and effectively embodies a commonplace truth based on practical experience or common sense."[7] Some common proverbs many of us have heard for years are "Early to bed and early to rise, makes a man healthy, wealthy, and wise." Or, "It's no use crying over spilled milk." We have grown up with sayings like these and we understand their purpose. They are attempts to concisely state a truth of some kind.

One of my mother's favorites was "An ounce of prevention is worth a pound of cure." I heard her recite this many times and the point was obvious. But it is also essential that we address what proverbs are not. They are not statements that are always true. Sometimes proverbs fail. For example, we can probably think of times we have attempted to prevent something—but achieved nothing. Yet we understand that preventative measures are important, and in general, "an ounce of prevention is worth a pound of cure."

Proverbs in the Bible are not intended to be legal guarantees. Rather, they state an observation about life in a succinct manner that tends to stick with us. Ironically, the more concise a principle is stated in a proverb, the more wisdom is required to unpack it and interpret it correctly. It is important when we turn to the book of Proverbs that we understand the nature of a proverb.

The Book of Proverbs

The book of Proverbs, then, is a collection of general

truths and observations about our world. For example, we are told in Proverbs, "Whoso findeth a wife findeth a good thing."[b] Is this always true? Most of us can think of a man who found a wife who was not a blessing to him at all. Yet there is an overriding truth in this verse. Many a man has found his wife to be a great blessing. This statement is a general observation about life.

Think about this verse: "The Lord will destroy the house of the proud: but he will establish the border of the widow."[c] But many a proud man has lived and died in his mansion, and it was never destroyed. This proverb is not intended to legally bind God to destroy the house of every proud man. But it is a concise saying that warns against the ultimate end of pride, and it tells us that God cares for the widows.

Or consider this familiar proverb. "A soft answer turneth away wrath."[d] Does it always? Jesus responded very kindly to His accusers, but they crucified Him anyway. Most of us have experienced situations where we received wrath in spite of our soft answers.

---

[b] Proverbs 18:22
[c] Proverbs 15:25
[d] Proverbs 15:1

But again, we understand the general truth in this verse. Those who answer with kindness instead of harshness tend to defuse angry confrontations.

The book of Proverbs is full of these kinds of observations. So what should we do with them? Are we to conclude that the book is untrustworthy since some of the statements do not apply to all situations? As we search for God's will concerning business, should we avoid the teachings of Proverbs?

Recently I met a Servant Sam who had come to this conclusion. Since the book of Proverbs is part of the Old Testament, he decided its counsel on wealth should be regarded the same way as God's promises of material blessing in Deuteronomy. Since it differs from Jesus' message, its teachings are no longer in effect and should not be used today.

I do not believe this is correct. Proverbs contains much practical advice that still applies today. But as with all Old Testament teachings, we need to be careful how we apply them.

The Formula for Material Success

Proverbs teaches how to make the material world work for us. It is the operating manual provided by the Manufacturer Himself. Men throughout the ages have applied its teachings to their lives, and many have become financially successful. When a young man needs teaching in diligence, or a newly married couple needs encouragement in financial management, we direct them to Proverbs. These principles are still true and still work thousands of years after they were first penned. The book of Proverbs contains the formula for material success, and many people have found provision for their natural needs by following its teachings.

Because it is the operating manual for the material world, the principles taught in Proverbs work regardless of a person's religion. The Japanese are not known for following the Bible, yet Japan is a wealthy country. How can this be? It is because its people have unknowingly lived out much of the message of Proverbs. The Japanese have a strong work ethic, are diligent in business, and are famous for their high personal savings rate. Though the average Japanese person may not be aware of the source, these foundational values from Scripture have made the country successful financially.

The Message of Jesus

But Jesus brought a different message. He didn't give business seminars or lectures on how people could increase their earthly wealth. If you go to His teachings hoping to find pointers on increasing business revenue, you won't find much, because that wasn't His mission. Jesus introduced an eternal kingdom and challenged us to aim higher than silver and gold. He taught that we should make every decision from an eternal perspective. He said a man who had nothing at the end of his life but earthly possessions was a fool. With authoritative teaching and powerful illustrations He showed us how to look at this material life in a radically different way.

Although Jesus' perspective on wealth was different from Proverbs, note that He never suggested that the truths in Proverbs are no longer valid. He didn't say, "Ye have heard it hath been said, 'He that tilleth his land shall have plenty of bread.' But I say unto you, don't get up so early to work in the field. Relax, God knows you need food and will bring it to you." Jesus didn't say it was impossible to accumulate earthly wealth by heeding Proverbs. He just taught that earthly wealth wasn't worth accumulating.

A central theme runs throughout Jesus' teachings regarding money and possessions: everything around us will soon be worthless. And since that day is quickly approaching, a wise man will view life, money, and possessions from an eternal perspective. Jesus wasn't saying that having a good work ethic, saving for known expenses, or being diligent in our business decisions wasn't beneficial. But He was saying that a man can do all of this and still be bankrupt at the end of life. Actually, the author of Proverbs also hinted at the foolishness of focusing only on material wealth. "There is that maketh himself rich, yet hath nothing: there is that maketh himself poor, yet hath great riches."[e] Even in the Old Testament there was a basic understanding that earthly wealth alone was insufficient, and Jesus persistently emphasized the folly of having an earthbound vision.

Most of us have grown up listening to the Sermon on the Mount. We hear what Jesus said, we discuss and try to understand what He really meant, and we memorize many of the passages. But remember,

---

[e] Proverbs 13:7

Jesus was talking to people who had been raised on the book of Proverbs and the Mosaic Law. I don't think we can comprehend the powerful impact His teachings had when they were first spoken. Imagine growing up in a setting where you are taught that God blesses materially those who are faithful to Him. And then Jesus comes along saying, "It is easier for a camel to go through the eye of a needle, than for a rich man to enter into the kingdom of God." No wonder the disciples were astonished. We would have been just as shocked as they were!

CHAPTER NINE

Reconciling Proverbs and Jesus

So what are we to do with the differences in focus and message? And how are we to apply these differences in our occupations? Although Proverbs and the teachings of Jesus have a different purpose and focus, they do not contradict each other. In fact, both are essential for operating a kingdom-focused business. Let's look at how both messages have powerful roles to play in our lives.

1. Proverbs provides the how—Jesus the why. Proverbs tells us *how* to produce income, and the teachings of Jesus tell us *why*. Proverbs provides the tools to make the material world work for us. We learn that it is important to get out of bed in the morning, that we need be out in the field/workplace to survive, and that we must plan ahead. In the New Testament we discover *why* God wants us to be involved in these activities. We are to use money to provide for our families,[a] to assist the fatherless and widows,[b] and to send aid to needy believers around the world.[c] None of this is possible without industry, and nothing surpasses Proverbs in teaching how to make business profitable. But what is the purpose behind this production and profit? Proverbs teaches how, and Jesus taught us why.

2. Money can be useful in furthering the kingdom. In some ways it would be easier if Jesus had just told us to stay away from money. Sometimes I see young people taking this position out of reaction. But Jesus didn't say this. In fact, He taught that, as dangerous as money is, it can be useful in the kingdom. One of the most lengthy

---

[a] 1 Timothy 5:8
[b] James 1:27
[c] 2 Corinthians 8:14

and difficult parables Jesus told was the story of the unjust steward.[d] Through the years men have wrestled to understand why Jesus used an unrighteous man to illustrate a godly concept. But the concluding message is clear. While we are not to serve money, it can be useful in furthering the kingdom of God. Paul picked up this theme in his letter to the church at Ephesus when he encouraged them to earn money so they would "have to give to him that needeth."[e]

3. Surrendering what is right and fair. Proverbs describes what is right and fair and has many teachings regarding cause and effect. If you do certain things, you can expect certain results. It describes what is just and reasonable, and every business owner should be familiar with it. But the teachings of Jesus take us far beyond the pursuit of what is right and fair. They call us to lay down our personal rights—to not insist on receiving what may be fair and equitable, and to consider each business transaction from the other person's perspective. Jesus doesn't disagree with the teachings in Proverbs describing fair treatment. He just taught us not to insist on it.

---

[d] Luke 16:1-12

[e] Ephesians 4:28

4. Wealth is to be accumulated. Both Proverbs and the teachings of Jesus encourage accumulation of wealth. But while Proverbs primarily focuses on the blessings that come from accumulating temporal wealth,[f] Jesus' teachings emphasize another kind of treasure and a different place to save. In contrast to temporal wealth, which is subject to moth, rust, and thieves, Jesus reveals a savings account surpassing any security measures man can provide.[g] He says we can direct-deposit into this heavenly account now. Imagine that! You can almost sense the excitement in Jesus' voice as He urges His listeners, "Sell that ye have, and give alms; provide yourselves bags which wax not old, a treasure in the heavens that faileth not, where no thief approacheth, neither moth corrupteth."[h] Business owners are interested in return on investment. There is no greater risk-free investment being offered today, and wise business owners will shift their assets to this heavenly account as quickly as possible.

---

[f] Proverbs 14:24
[g] Matthew 6:19
[h] Luke 12:33

The book of Proverbs contains the universal building blocks to help us provide for our families. I can think of no better resource for a young man who wants to understand how to make the material world work for him. It will teach him to work hard and plan ahead, and it will provide the principles for successful business operation. Everyone should become familiar with its teachings. But in the middle of all our hustle and bustle, it is essential to stop and ask *why* diligence and a good work ethic are so important. Proverbs and the teachings of Jesus are intended to complement each other.

An entrepreneur loves logic, challenge, production, and common sense, and the business world naturally rewards the man who pursues these attributes.

> A man who lives only by the teachings of Proverbs can die a fool!

Consequently, Christians who enjoy business can become enamored with the Biblical truths in Proverbs and give less attention to the call of Jesus. Beware! A man who lives only by the teachings of Proverbs can die a fool![i]

---

[i] Luke 12:21

CHAPTER TEN

The Kingdom at Work

M ost businessmen can easily wrap their minds around the common-sense teachings of Proverbs. But what about the teachings of Jesus and the apostles? Paul reiterated Jesus' view when he told the church at Corinth, "Let no man seek his own, but every man another's wealth."[a] How can a man

---

[a] 1 Corinthians 10:24

operate a profitable business while doing this, and what does a kingdom business look like?

Let's look at some elementary business principles. Whether you sell sweet corn at the end of your lane or own a large company with many employees, there are some basic Biblical principles that apply.

1. The kingdom of God is to be first. Jesus was clear that we must first seek the kingdom of God.[b] This foundational truth is easily forgotten amid the constant stress and pressure of business life, and we need to be reminded often. Following Jesus is to be first, and every other passion and pursuit must be under His control. "Whosoever he be of you who forsaketh not all that he hath," Jesus said, "he cannot be my disciple."[c] Jesus calls us to surrender everything and follow Him, even if it means abandoning family relationships. Since Jesus calls us to place our families on the altar, we must place our businesses there as well.

The New Testament commands us to labor and

---

[b] Matthew 6:33
[c] Luke 14:33

provide for our families.[d] But sometimes that can become an excuse for selfish business ambitions. God has given men a desire to make things work—an inner craving to produce and provide. This is good and normal, and we become concerned when this is absent in a man's life. But this inner desire, which God meant for good, becomes a snare when outside the lordship of Jesus Christ. We need to daily reexamine our values. Jesus said that one soul is worth more than the entire world.[e] Do I really believe this? Would someone watching my business transactions each day say I believe it? The kingdom of God must be primary in our lives, and we need to be called back to this truth daily.

2. God still cares about "all these things." A cursory reading of the teachings of Jesus might cause you to conclude that God no longer blesses materially—that in Old Testament times God blessed His people with earthly things, but now His only blessings are spiritual. While it is true that Jesus warned against wealth, taught that it is extremely difficult

---

[d] 1 Timothy 5:8
[e] Matthew 16:26

for a rich man to enter heaven, and cautioned us not to worry about our physical needs, we must remember that God still provides for us materially. After strongly admonishing us not to worry about what we will eat, drink, or wear, Jesus said, "But seek ye first the kingdom of God, and his righteousness; and all these things shall be added unto you."[f] God hasn't forgotten about our natural needs. He made us and understands that we need food and clothing to survive. This verse isn't saying that God will supply all our wants. But it does promise that He will be with us and provide for our needs.

3. We are to hold possessions loosely. Many believers throughout history have been called to live in poverty, and many today are willing to live in difficult conditions to follow Jesus. I met a young girl in Indonesia who was raised Muslim, and her choice to follow Jesus had disrupted her entire life. She was searching for a community where no one would recognize her because her immediate family would kill her if she was found. She didn't know how she was going to survive. But Jesus cares about

---

[f] Matthew 6:33

these situations and is well able to provide. "Verily I say unto you, There is no man that hath left house, or brethren, or sisters, or father, or mother, or wife, or children, or lands, for my sake, and the gospel's, but he shall receive an hundredfold now in this time, houses, and brethren, and sisters, and mothers, and children, and lands, with persecutions; and in the world to come eternal life."[g]

Many believers in restricted countries could attest to the truth of this promise. They have walked away from earthly resources and relationships, and in exchange God has provided new friends, homes with open doors, and meals around tables with people who care. So let's follow Jesus in faith. Let's place our business decisions in His care. He knows we have material needs and is well able to provide all these physical things.

4. Multiplication is of God. Several years ago I was asked to speak about finances to a group of pastors in Ukraine. Afterward, a pastor in the back of the room stood and asked, "Can you show me a verse in the Bible that tells us it is right for a

---

[g] Mark 10:29, 30

business to make a profit on a sale?" I have been asked many questions after financial seminars, but this was a new one! Acceptable to make a profit in business? I have never heard that question in North America. To appreciate the question, we must understand the setting. These pastors had been raised under communism. The government was supposed to supply all their needs, though it rarely did. The only individuals involved in commerce were criminals operating in the black market. These undercover merchants preyed on the poor who lacked daily necessities, charging exorbitant prices for their products. Consequently, the Ukrainian church now believed it was wrong to sell a product for more than its purchase price.

Jesus didn't teach that it was wrong to earn a profit. In fact, all through His teachings you find the opposite. Many of His teachings, His miracles, and even nature demonstrate that profit, or increase, is of God. How many of us would plant one seed of corn if we knew at harvest time we would only get one seed in return? Multiplication is a basic principle in nature and it tells us something about the character of God. In fact, "be fruitful and multiply"[h] was one of His first commands. It is obvious that God loves increase!

Consider how God has revealed this truth about Himself in Scripture. In one parable, a man was upbraided for not at least putting his money in the bank to earn interest. In the same account, others were praised for multiplying the investment that had been entrusted to them. Jesus multiplied the five loaves and two fishes and at one point caused the disciples' nets to break from a huge catch of fish. Jesus was not opposed to increase. But He wants us to understand that increase is of God.

Sometimes we react to others' selfish use of their profits and develop improper conclusions. Like the Ukrainian pastor, we become so intent on avoiding one ditch that we end up in another. God intends that our fields and factories produce a profit.

5. Much shall be required. As those profits increase, so does our responsibility as stewards of what the Lord has given us. "For unto whomsoever much

---

[h] Genesis 1:28

is given, of him shall be much required."[i] We live in an amazing time. America represents only about 5 percent of the world's population, yet it controls 45 percent of the wealth.[8] Never in the history of man has there been such disparity in the world or such opportunity in one country. Those of us who grew up in this environment often fail to appreciate the blessing we have been given. If you live under a stable government or have steady employment, you have a tremendous opportunity. Compared to global reality, you have been blessed abundantly!

[i] Luke 12:48

CHAPTER ELEVEN

Attributes of a Kingdom Business

It should be obvious that a business operating under the kingship of Jesus Christ is going to function differently than a secular business. It will respond differently to a customer's concerns and will view success from a different perspective. A kingdom business deals with customers, vendors, and employees in a different way. Not just as pawns to increase revenue and profitability, but as individuals with souls who have been made in the image of God. All this will directly impact daily operations. Let's take a closer look at some ways in which a kingdom business will operate differently than a secular one.

1. It seeks the good of others. Early in Jesus' ministry He said, "As ye would that men should do to you, do ye also to them likewise."[a] We have our children memorize this principle and rightly tell them that living it out will help them avoid many squabbles with their playmates. But this basic teaching should permeate every part of our lives. A business owner will be concerned about the welfare of his employees and will ensure they are properly cared for and are receiving fair wages. He will treat them the way he himself would want to be treated.

This principle will also affect how we treat and speak about the competition. When potential customers ask about our competitors, we will speak of them in the same way we would want them to talk about us. We would want others to be honest about our products or services, but also share facts in the best light possible. This can be difficult to live

---

[a] Luke 6:31

out, but we need to keep reminding ourselves of our goal—we want our business to represent Jesus Himself. The kingdom of God must be primary, and seeking the good of others is one of the most lacking Biblical principles in Christian businesses today.

2. It pursues win-win transactions. Recently I entered a local hardware store to buy a tube of silicone. I took it up to the counter, and the clerk informed me that it would cost me about four dollars. I had four dollars in my pocket. I would have liked to keep my money, but at that moment I wanted that silicone more than the four dollars. And the hardware store wanted my four dollars more than that tube of silicone. The exchange was made, and both of us were happy as we parted. That is healthy commerce.

But why did that tube of silicone cost four dollars? If that hardware store operates like most businesses, they charged four dollars because they thought that was the highest price I would be willing to pay for it. The price is based on a market-based equilibrium, with the seller closely calculating how he can extract the most money from the buyer and produce the most income. This is how the capitalistic business culture generally works. But a kingdom-focused business will use more than just potential profits to determine pricing. We also want to ensure that the other person is receiving what he needs in the exchange.

I can think of many Christian businessmen who exemplify this virtue—men I do business with who always give a little more, charge a little less, or in some way exceed my expectations. I come to them with a picture in my mind of what I want to receive and what it should cost, and somehow they manage to provide more for less.

Growing up, I heard stories about a farmer I will call Alvin. It was well known in his community that if you were doing business with Alvin you needed to keep your eye on him. If you bought hay, you'd better watch the tally. He seemed to find ways to slip extra bales over to your side when you weren't looking. I remember stories from men who share-cropped with him. Alvin had all kinds of creative ways to make sure others got the best end of a deal. Alvin has been gone for many years, yet people still talk about him. I believe a healthy church or community should be full of people like this, each trying to secretly bless the other as they interact and transact business. Paul calls this being a cheerful giver, and I like to imagine church communities filled with people like Alvin.[b]

Earlier we said that increase is of God. A follower of Jesus, however, will not base every decision solely on how it will affect him, his company, or his bottom line. He will also give thought to what is best for the other person. The Apostle Paul told the church at Corinth, "Let no man seek his own, but every man another's wealth."[c] A kingdom-focused businessman will be driven by more than just potential income. He will also aim to bless his customers in every transaction.

3. Its activities intentionally glorify God. "Let your light so shine before men," Jesus said, "that they may see your good works, and glorify your Father which is in heaven."[d] Live your life and conduct your activities in such a way that those looking on will be inspired to turn toward God. This simple command should permeate all our business activities.

---

[b] 2 Corinthians 9:7
[c] 1 Corinthians 10:24
[d] Matthew 5:16

One time when I was working on a construction site, I came into a room just as the general contractor had left. The owner was lingering in the room after their meeting, staring out a window at the man's receding figure. Pointing toward the contractor, he turned to me and said with emotion, "That man is the closest imitation of Jesus Christ I have ever met."

I have no idea what they had been discussing. But whatever had occurred, that contractor had conducted himself in such a Christ-like manner that his customer was astonished. Living out what Jesus taught will impact how we treat our customers, respond to vendors, and fulfill our contracts. It will cause us to speak, act, and respond generously in daily life. And the man who is dedicated to following Jesus in business will find himself basing every decision on whether or not it glorifies his Father in heaven.

4. Profitability is sought, not promised. All of us understand that a business cannot operate long-term without profitability. But a kingdom business will always keep profitability under obedience to King Jesus. There will be times when those two pursuits clash, and when this occurs, profit must be subservient. When we choose to follow Jesus, we relinquish our right to earthly wealth. We give up our right to what Proverbs tells us is fair and just, and our new goal is to live for Christ and His kingdom. And that isn't a motto that most business owners go by. Business is famous for being a self-centered pursuit. Profit is front and center. So, are the teachings of Jesus compatible with the modern business world? Or to put it more bluntly, if Jesus tried to operate a business in the dog-eat-dog environment of our day, would He go broke?

If you are a Christian businessman, you have probably wrestled with this question. Jesus' teachings are radical, and at times they seem almost incompatible with financial survival. Yet I assure you that there are many (though not as many as there should be) businesses that are being operated by Christian principles. It *is* possible to follow Jesus and be financially successful, and I have observed many who apply His teachings daily in their business dealings. They are public demonstrations that Jesus' teachings are not incompatible with their occupations. And the problems they experience and the ways they respond provide excellent opportunities to demonstrate powerful truths.

But I have also seen believers suffer great loss because they put kingdom values ahead of common business practice. Choosing to operate your business using the teachings of Jesus does not ensure profitability. There will be times when you need to decide which is more important. Am I going to allow Jesus or profit to rule in this situation? Will I keep Christ on the throne even when the financial loss will be great? As mentioned earlier, profit itself is not wrong. But neither is profit to be the only purpose in our businesses.

> "Am I going to allow Jesus or profit to rule in this situation?"

5. It will create curiosity about Christ. A few years ago I was talking to a small business owner who, from my observation, had intentionally reached out to his customers. So I asked him to describe the vision he has for his business. He listed several goals, but one of them jumped out at me. "I want everyone who walks out of my store to leave with a curiosity about Christ." I left that day inspired by his vision. He wasn't just hanging up a sign about Jesus, leaving a few tracts on the counter, or putting a fish symbol on his business card. Rather, he was intentionally interacting with his customers in such a way that when they left they would feel blessed and would be thinking, *I would really like to know more about the God these people serve!*

I was inspired even more as I expanded that vision. What if every business owner in his congregation and all their believing employees shared that same goal? What kind of impact would that have on the community? How might this affect their neighbors' perception of Christianity? And further, how much impact might embracing this goal have on everyday choices that have to be made, and even on Sunday morning attendance?

CHAPTER TWELVE

Business Dilemmas— Kingdom Perspective

George owned a small construction company. A man who enjoyed hunting big game around the globe asked him to construct a building to show off his trophy animals. George began the project, and everything was going well. The site work was finished and the concrete slab poured when small cracks began developing all over the slab. The owner noticed these fissures and asked George about them.

George wasn't sure, so he contacted the concrete contractor and the ready-mix supplier in an effort to determine the cause of the problem.

The concrete contractor and supplier came to a meeting, but both immediately pointed fingers at the other. One said the concrete hadn't been finished correctly, and the other insisted the product had been deficient from the start. At the conclusion of the meeting, nothing had been decided. Everyone proclaimed his innocence—and the concrete was still cracked. Since the concrete wasn't structural and would be covered with carpet, both said the issue wasn't that important anyway.

Within a few days George received another call from the owner, who wasn't happy about the situation. He agreed that the tiny cracks in the concrete were not really that important, but he didn't like the idea of paying the full price for an inferior product. He said that since George was the general contractor, he was going to sue him to get even with the ready-mix supplier and the concrete contractor.

The Ultimate Goal

George, more than anything else, wanted his business

to glorify God. As he talked to the owner, he shared his faith in Christ and his desire to be known for honesty and integrity. He described the reproach that involvement in a public lawsuit might have on his Christian witness in the community. But none of this moved the owner. He had paid good money for this concrete and couldn't stand the thought of the supplier and contractor getting off free.

George would have loved to simply refund part of what the owner had paid, but he had a young family and few financial resources to draw from. So he made a proposal. He asked the owner if there was anything he could do for him personally to resolve the situation, maybe something extra on the building he could do free of charge. The owner thought about this and finally said there was. He needed to build a small pump house, and if George would construct this for him at no charge, he would be satisfied. So that's what George agreed to do. The next Saturday found him at the project site early in the morning working on the pump house.

This went on for several Saturdays. One morning the owner stopped by to see how things were going. He talked to George for a while and then exclaimed,

"George, this isn't right! You are out here working for nothing, and the men who created this problem are not paying a thing! This isn't fair, and the concrete problem isn't that big a deal anyway. When you get done building this, I want you to send me a bill for your time and the materials."

George's primary desire was that the Lord would be glorified by his business dealings, and he was willing to lose money to make this happen. If he had shown any resistance, there would have been court costs, and the owner could have made George's life miserable for the duration of the project. But by following Jesus and staying true to his vision of living for the kingdom, he not only kept his Christian witness, but he also built a strong relationship with the owner. As an added blessing, he even got paid for his efforts.

It is amazing how often God materially blesses individuals who choose to take the path of Jesus. But will situations always turn out like George's? Of course not. Many business owners have sustained huge losses by choosing to follow Jesus' teachings.

Experiencing Loss

Jack Phillips is the owner of Masterpiece Cakeshop in

Lakewood, Colorado. In 2012, Phillips refused to bake a wedding cake for David Mullins and Charlie Craig because he doesn't believe gay marriage is Biblical. Consequently, these two men took Jack Phillips to court, claiming discrimination against their sexual orientation. Phillips testified that he would be willing to sell cupcakes for a birthday party for someone who is gay, but said, "I don't want to participate in a same-sex wedding."[9] The court ruled against Phillips, and his initial response was to cease making wedding cakes. Wedding cakes at that time represented approximately 40% of his revenue,[10] so this represented a huge loss for his business. Four years later the US Supreme Court reversed this decision, but Jack's problems weren't over. He later ended up in court for refusing to bake a birthday cake celebrating a potential customer's transition from male to female.[11]

George ended up gaining financially because of his decision to follow Jesus, but Jack Phillips didn't. In Paul's letter to the church at Corinth, he implied that when we choose to follow Jesus we might at times be defrauded and taken advantage of.[a] When

---

[a] 1 Corinthians 6:7

we choose to follow Jesus, we need to understand this possibility.

Could Jesus be successful as a businessman in our world? Absolutely! His teachings are not incompatible with business. Many could testify how His teachings have helped them resolve conflicts with customers, develop a loyal customer base, and even receive payment on overdue bills. But in asking this question we must reexamine our definition of success. If our primary motive is large profits, there is little in the New Testament that guarantees increased income to the Christian. But if our primary desire is to provide for our families, assist those in need, and portray Christ to the world through our businesses, we can move forward in confidence. Jesus is calling businessmen everywhere to place their personal business ambitions on the altar and make their Father's business their first priority.

CHAPTER THIRTEEN

Needed: Real-Life Illustrations

A warm, gentle breeze drifts in through the open windows. The Sunday morning service is halfway over, the sermon a little monotonous, and the topic failing to connect. Several older men begin to nod, little boys gaze longingly out the window, and the mother who finally got her infant to sleep fights her own drowsiness. A fly buzzes in vain against the window pane and a spirit of sleepy indifference slowly creeps over the congregation as the minister patiently tries to regain the attention of his drowsy flock. All of us have been there.

Suddenly everything changes. "Let me tell you a story to illustrate my point," the minister announces. The men sit up, little boys expectantly refocus on the speaker, and even that little girl (the one you assumed hadn't even been listening) is suddenly alert. There is something about a story that captivates and enthralls.

We can understand why Jesus used stories so prolifically throughout his ministry. I am intrigued with the power of stories and their ability to draw us in. Recently while in South Sudan I was struck by the comment of an extremely poor illiterate South Sudanese woman. "We learn the most from living stories," she said. This woman had heard good doctrinal teaching, she was telling me, but she learned the most from watching someone live out the principle in real life, or at least hearing a story about it.

We like illustrations, particularly stories we can identify with, and we learn the most when observing real-life examples. This is also true in the area of Biblical stewardship and kingdom business. While teaching on this topic is important, what we really need are more real-life demonstrations. We need authentic Christian businessmen. Men who have consecrated every part of their lives to Jesus.

The Spiritual/Secular Divide

We have a tendency to separate the spiritual from the secular. Reading our Bibles, praying, going to church—these are seen as spiritual. But our occupations, paying the bills, and all the activity required to provide for our families is seen as secular and less important. Sometimes we think our spiritual lives would be more vibrant if we didn't have to go to work each day. We would have plenty of time to help our neighbors whenever they have a need, and we would be able to involve ourselves in all kinds of "spiritual" activities, unrestricted by the cares of this life.

Believers have wrestled with thoughts like this for many years, and some have concluded that following Jesus means putting as much distance as possible between themselves and money or business. In fact, some have concluded that believers should return to bartering and totally avoid using money. Books have been written on the evils of the current monetary structure, and some speak of withdrawing from the banking system that the developed world employs. But I invite you to rethink with me our view of business and occupational life. Is it possible that God has more in mind for our businesses and occupations than we have understood?

The Untapped Power in Business

Our lives can become unbalanced. It is very possible, especially in an affluent, consumer-driven society, to place undue focus on our occupations while neglecting personal time with God. But it is also possible to miss the powerful potential that God has in our occupations. It's easy to forget that God desires our businesses to be living illustrations to a lost world of what the kingdom of God looks like. More than just talking about the power of Christianity, we need businessmen whose lives have actually been transformed—men who are not enamored by wealth or the trappings of a materialistic society.

We need men like Moses. He could have had anything he desired, but he turned his back on earthly wealth and power and chose instead to live for the glory of God. We need men who, as the Apostle Paul, throw all their energy into God's kingdom and count everything else "but loss for the excellency of the knowledge of Christ Jesus"[a]—all the while continuing to make tents.[b]

We need more transformed men who sense God's call to serve Him in the workplace. Men who see their businesses as missions in the marketplace. Businessmen who purposefully use commerce as a platform to display the glory and superiority of the kingdom of God. Paul had such an aspiration for the church at Philippi. He desired that they interact within their culture "without rebuke, in the midst of a crooked and perverse nation, among whom ye shine as lights in the world."[c] That is still God's will for us today.

> We need more transformed men who sense God's call to serve Him in the workplace.

---

[a] Philippians 3:8
[b] Acts 18:3
[c] Philippians 2:15

Does earthly wealth intrigue you? Do you find yourself enamored with the temporal? Do you at times question whether trying to swim against an ungodly value system is worth it? If so, there is a man in the Bible who identified with your struggle. Asaph the psalm writer found himself envying the ungodly and feeling jealous of the wealthy. He wondered why everything seemed to go so well for those who blasphemed the name of the Lord and ignored His Word. But Asaph struggled with such thoughts only until he went into the sanctuary of God and came to understand their end.[d] What changed in the sanctuary? He saw God! And when a man sees God for who He really is and compares God's values with his own, it has a drastic impact on his perspective!

A Time to Abandon Our Career

After a seminar a few years ago, I was approached by a wealthy businessman. He felt he had no option but to occasionally use the court system. His question was, "Do you think in my situation it would be okay to use a lawsuit to get people to pay? If I don't, I won't be able to stay in business." I would

---

[d] Psalm 73:17

suggest that this man was asking the wrong question. The question should have been, "Can I demonstrate the kingdom of God while I am taking people to court?" This question should be at the center of these dilemmas.

While business offers a tremendous opportunity to display Jesus' teachings, it also provides a strong temptation to abandon kingdom values. If you continually struggle to maintain a proper perspective in business, you may need to abandon your career. Jesus called for extreme measures when dealing with distractions, regardless of the cost. If there are situations that call for removal of a right hand or an eye,[e] surely a vocational change isn't out of the question. All of us will struggle at times to keep our perspective. When this occurs, go back and analyze your connection with God. Getting close to God has always changed a man's perspective. It still does!

Mission in the Marketplace
I don't know what kind of business paradigm you operate under or how much thought you have given to using your business as a mission. Maybe you have

---

[e] Matthew 5:29, 30

assumed giving a portion of your profit is really all God is looking for. But I want to challenge you to aim higher. Resolve to use the marketplace to demonstrate something greater. Intentionally put your occupation on the altar and let the power of the Lord Jesus control your decisions. Not only will you impact unbelievers, but other Christians will also be inspired to examine their foundational reasons for being in business.

There is a mission field right where you are, and Jesus is looking for those who will trust Him and surrender their wills when making daily business decisions. So go forth in His power. Remember, it's not your business, but the Lord's. Let the teachings of Proverbs inspire you to diligence and instruct you as you manage your finances. But ultimately, allow the teachings of Jesus to be your primary reference point. Resolve to make decisions from His perspective. If you do so, your occupational life will provide a public demonstration. It will be an open exhibit of what commerce could be like if every businessman were a Christian, and what our world would be like if everyone chose to make Jesus Christ King of Kings!

Endnotes

Chapter Four

[1] William Lee Miller, *Arguing About Slavery: The Great Battle in the United States Congress,* Vintage Books, New York, 1996, p. 139.

[2] Marci A. Hamilton, *God vs. the Gavel,* Cambridge University Press, Cambridge, NY, 2005, p. 60.

[3] Norman H. Baynes (ed.), *The Speeches of Adolf Hitler, April 1922-August 1939,* Vol. 1, Oxford University Press, 1942, pp. 19-20.

Chapter Five

[4] List25 Team, "Joel Osteen Net Worth," List 25, <https://list25.com/joel-osteen-net-worth/>, accessed on 7/24/19.

[5] Joel Osteen, "World Vision," WV Artists, <http://www.wvartists.org/artist-detail/175127/joel-osteen/>, accessed on 6/5/14.

Chapter Six

[6] Ramsey Solutions, "About Dave," <http://www.daveramsey.com/careers/about-dave/>, accessed on 11/6/19.

Chapter Eight

[7] Literary Devices: Definitions and Examples of Literary Terms, "Proverb," <https://literarydevices.net/proverb/>, accessed on 7/1/19.

Chapter Ten

[8] Inequality, "Global Inequality," <https://inequality.org/facts/global-inequality/>, accessed on 7/24/19.

Chapter Twelve

[9] CBS News, "Colorado baker to stop making wedding cakes . . ." May 31, 2014, <http://www.cbsnews.com/news/colorado-baker-to-stop-making-wedding-cakes-after-losing-discrimination-case/>, accessed on 6/9/14.

[10] Alliance Defending Freedom, "Masterpiece Cakeshop v. Colorado Civil Rights Commission," <http://www.adfmedia.org/news/prdetail/8700>, accessed on 7/23/19.

[11] Michael Gryboski, "Jack Phillips faces third lawsuit . . ." *ChristianPost.com,* <https://www.christianpost.com/news/jack-phillips-faces-third-lawsuit-over-refusal-make-lgbt-gender-transition-cake.html>, accessed on 7/23/19.

About the Author

Gary Miller was raised in California and today lives with his wife Patty and family in the Pacific Northwest. Gary works with the poor in developing countries and directs the SALT Microfinance Solutions program for Christian Aid Ministries. This program offers business and spiritual teaching to those living in chronic poverty, provides small loans, sets up local village savings groups, and assists them in learning how to use their God-given resources to become sustainable.

Gary has authored the Kingdom-Focused Living series, microfinance manuals, and several booklets for outreach purposes. For a list of his books, see pages 125-130.

Have you been inspired by Gary's materials? Maybe you have questions, or perhaps you even disagree with the author. Share your thoughts by sending an e-mail to kingdomfinance@camoh.org or writing to Christian Aid Ministries, P.O. Box 360, Berlin, Ohio 44610.

Additional Books by Gary Miller

Kingdom-Focused Finances for the Family

This first book in the Kingdom-Focused Living series is realistic, humorous, and serious about getting us to become stewards instead of owners.

Charting a Course in Your Youth

A serious call to youth to examine their faith, focus, and finances. Second book in Kingdom-Focused Living series.

Going Till You're Gone

A plea for godly examples—for older men and women who will demonstrate a kingdom-focused vision all the way to the finish line. Third book in Kingdom-Focused Living series.

The Other Side of the Wall

Stresses Biblical principles that apply to all Christians who want to reflect God's heart in giving. Applying these principles has the potential to change lives—first our own, and then the people God calls us to share with. Fourth book in Kingdom-Focused Living series.

It's Not Your Business

How involved in business should followers of Jesus be? Did God intend the workplace to play a prominent role in building his kingdom? Explore the benefits and dangers in business. Fifth and final book in the Kingdom-Focused Living series.

Budgeting Made Simple

A budgeting workbook in a ring binder; complements *Kingdom-Focused Finances for the Family.*

What Happened to Our Money?

Ignorance of Biblical money management can set young people on a path of financial hardship that results in anxiety, marital discord, depression, and envy. This short book presents foundational truths on which young couples can build their financial lives.

Life in a Global Village

Would your worldview change if the world population were shrunk to a village of one hundred people and you lived in that village? Full-color book.

This Side of the Global Wall

Pictures and graphs in this full-color book portray the unprecedented opportunities Americans have today. What are we doing with the resources God has given us?

Small Business Handbook

A manual used in microfinance programs in developing countries. Includes devotionals and practical business teaching. Ideal for missions and churches.

Following Jesus in Everyday Life

A teaching manual ideal for mission settings. Each lesson addresses a Biblical principle and includes a story and discussion questions. Black and white illustrations.

A Good Soldier of Jesus Christ

A teaching manual like *Following Jesus in Everyday Life*, but targeting youth.

Know Before You Go

Every year, thousands of Americans travel to distant countries to help the needy. But could some of these short-term mission trips be doing more harm than good? This book encourages us to reexamine our goals and methods, and prepares people to effectively interact with other cultures in short-term missions.

Jesus Really Said That?

This book presents five teachings of Jesus that are often missed, ignored, or rejected. It tells the story of Jeremy and Alicia, a couple who thought they understood Christianity and knew what it meant to be a Christian . . . until they began to look at what Jesus actually said!

Radical Islam

From the barbarous actions of ISIS to the shocking tactics of Al-Qaida, radical Islamic extremists seem to be everywhere and growing stronger. Many wonder in alarm if the movement will overtake the West and change Americans' way of life forever. How should Christians respond to this threat? Does the Bible have answers? How would Jesus respond?

How Can Anyone Say God Is Good?

Nick is fed up with life and aggravated by the simpleminded people who believe in a supreme being in spite of all the agony and chaos around them. How can they have the audacity to say their God is good? Written in story form and ending with the author's personal journey, this book is a good gift for an agnostic or atheist friend. It can also be used to strengthen the faith of a Christian believer.

Church Matters

How can we increase the impact of our churches on the world around us? Why do we struggle to be a light to the world? Are splits and disagreements okay? Compare the current state of the church with God's original vision in the book of Acts. This book will challenge your Christian life and possibly your ideology of the church.

Surviving the Tech Tsunami

Electronic technology is taking our culture by storm and is tremendously impacting our occupations, our families, our personal lives, and also our churches. This behind-the-scenes glimpse at the cultural upheaval caused by technology should serve as a sober wakeup call and help our families and churches weather the tech tsunami.

About Christian Aid Ministries

Christian Aid Ministries was founded in 1981 as a nonprofit, tax-exempt 501(c)(3) organization. Its primary purpose is to provide a trustworthy and efficient channel for Amish, Mennonite, and other conservative Anabaptist groups and individuals to minister to physical and spiritual needs around the world. This is in response to the command to ". . . do good unto all men, especially unto them who are of the household of faith" (Galatians 6:10).

Each year, CAM supporters provide 15-20 million pounds of food, clothing, medicines, seeds, Bibles, Bible story books, and other Christian literature for needy people. Most of the aid goes to orphans and Christian families. Supporters' funds also help to clean up and rebuild for natural disaster victims, put up Gospel billboards in the U.S., support several church-planting efforts, operate two medical clinics, and provide resources for needy families to make their own living. CAM's main purposes for providing aid are to help and encourage God's people and bring the Gospel to a lost and dying world.

CAM has staff, warehouses, and distribution networks in Romania, Moldova, Ukraine, Haiti, Nicaragua, Liberia, Israel, and Kenya. Aside from management, supervisory personnel, and bookkeeping operations, volunteers do most of the work at CAM locations. Each year, volunteers at our warehouses, field bases, Disaster Response Services projects, and other locations donate over 200,000 hours of work.

CAM's ultimate purpose is to glorify God and help enlarge His kingdom. ". . . whatsoever ye do, do all to the glory of God" (1 Corinthians 10:31).